FLAG FOOTBALL

BY KARA L. LAUGHLIN

The Child's World®
childsworld.com

Published by The Child's World®
1980 Lookout Drive • Mankato, MN 56003-1705
800-599-READ • www.childsworld.com

ACKNOWLEDGMENTS
The Child's World®: Mary Swensen, Publishing Director
The Design Lab: Design
Heidi Hogg: Editing
Sarah M. Miller: Editing

PHOTO CREDITS
© Andrew Rich/iStockphoto.com: 19; BluIz60/iStockphoto.com:
16, 20; Gary Paul Lewis/Shutterstock.com: cover, 1, 4, 15; Glen
Jones/Shutterstock.com: 10; James Steidl/Dreamstime.com: 9;
RTimages/Shutterstock.com: 2-3; Shawn Pecor/Shutterstock.com:
7, 13

ISBN: 9781503807754
LCCN: 2015958112

Printed in the United States of America
Mankato, MN
June, 2016
PA02300

TABLE OF CONTENTS

Time to Play!

The sky is clear. The air is crisp. It is a great day for flag football.

Equipment

You will need a field, a football, and a flag football **belt**.

The belt goes on top of your clothes. Cloth strips, or flags, hang from the belt.

Fast Fact!
Flags can be made of strong fabric or plastic. Some people even use socks or small towels!

Starting the Game

The game starts with a coin flip. The winner chooses who gets the ball. The team with the ball is the **offense**. The other team is the **defense**.

Fast Fact!
Flag football became popular in the 1940s.

9

Rushing

The offense lines up. They **snap** the ball to the **quarterback**. The defense rushes toward him. They are after his flag. If they can get it, they stop the ball.

Runs and Passes

The quarterback might run. He might also throw a **pass**. A player catches the pass! She runs until someone grabs her flag.

13

Huddles

Between plays, the teams **huddle**. They need to plan their next **play**. They line up where the last play stopped. When on offense, a team gets a few tries to get the ball to the **end zone**.

Fast Fact!
Some flag football teams wear helmets and pads. Many do not.

The defense can catch a pass, too. The player runs down the field with the ball. She can even run it to the end zone.

Fast Fact!
It is important to wear good running shoes when playing flag football.

Touchdown!

A team gets six points for a **touchdown**. They get one more play for extra points. Then the other team gets the ball.

Fast Fact!
The extra points in flag football are earned by passing or running the ball, not by kicking.

Each game has two halves. The teams switch sides after the first half. At the end of the game, the team with the most points wins.

Fast Fact!
There are more than 20 million flag football players in the United States.

Glossary

belt (BELT): Flags are attached to a belt with hook and loop patches. Every player wears a belt, and players pull off a flag to stop the ball.

defense (DEE-fenss): The team who is trying to keep the other team from scoring. They are defending their end zone.

end zone (END ZOHN): The area at each end of the field where teams can score a touchdown is called the end zone.

huddle (HUD-dul): A team gathers closely in a huddle to talk about their next play.

offense (OFF-enss): The team who is trying to score. They have the ball at the beginning of a play.

pass (PASS): Getting the football from one player to another. A lot of the time, a pass is thrown.

play (PLAY): A play is a team's plan for how to move the ball down the field.

quarterback (KWAR-ter-bak): The team member who gets the ball at the start of a play. He can run the ball or pass it to another player.

snap (SNAP): The way the quarterback gets the ball. A player holds the ball and hands or tosses it back to the quarterback.

touchdown (TUCH-down): The act of getting the football into the end zone. A touchdown is worth six points.

To Learn More

In the Library

Heller, Alyson. *Touchdown!* New York,
NY: Simon Spotlight, 2010.

Jacobs, Greg. *The Everything Kids' Football
Book.* Avon, MA: Adams Media, 2014.

Sports Illustrated Kids. *My First Book of Football.*
New York, NY: Time Inc. Books, 2015.

On the Web

Visit our Web site for links about flag football:
childsworld.com/links

Note to Parents, Teachers, and Librarians: We routinely verify
our Web links to make sure they are safe and active sites.
So encourage your readers to check them out!

Index

About the Author

Kara L. Laughlin is an artist and writer who lives in Virginia with her husband, three kids, two guinea pigs, and a dog. She is the author of two dozen nonfiction books for kids.